The children are waiting for a bus.
Miss Beech is with them.

They all have big bags. They all
chatter happily except Seth. He
stands and looks at the ground.

The bus comes and the children and Miss Beech get on it.

They get off the bus
at the swimming pool.

Martin, the instructor, tells the children to get into the pool. They jump in.

Seth hangs back.

"Come on Seth!" shouts Martin.
"Hurry up and get in the pool."

Seth is not a good swimmer.
He still needs floats.

"Kick your legs," Martin tells the children. There is a lot of splashing.

Seth tries not to get splashed.
Next the children swim across
the pool and back again.

They do lots of things in the swimming lesson – mushroom floats, star floats, and picking up rings from the bottom of the pool.

Martin tells the children to
swim up to the deep end.
Seth stands and shivers.

Then suddenly Ben cries
"Look! Seth is swimming!"

The children, Miss Beech
and Martin all clap.
Seth feels very proud.